For Marlon, Angela, Theodora, Alexandra, Ella, Orson, Ida, Ava, and Otto

—KR

To my family

—TR

A Note about the Story and Audio:

The song mentioned in this book, "Malagueña," was written by Ernesto Lecuona (1895–1963), a noted Cuban musician, conductor, and composer. You can learn more about Ernesto Lecuona and "Malagueña" at lecuona.com. Keith Richards's grandfather thought "Malagueña" was the perfect foundation for learning the guitar because it uses a finger-style technique that contributes crucially to developing a guitarist's tone. The enclosed audio includes only a brief excerpt of the song, and readers are encouraged to listen to the entire song and learn how to play it!

Copyright © 2014 by Mindless Records, LLC • Cover art by Theodora Richards • Back cover photograph by Jane Rose • Cover design by Gail Doobinin • Cover © 2014 Hachette Book Group, Inc. • MALAGUENA by Ernesto Lecuona. Used by permission of Edward B. Marks Music Company (BMI) • All rights reserved. In accordance with the U.S. Copyright Act of 1976, the scanning, uploading, and electronic sharing of any part of this book without the permission of the publisher is unlawful piracy and theft of the author's intellectual property. If you would like to use material from the book (other than for review purposes), prior written permission must be obtained by contacting the publisher at permissions@hbgusa.com. Thank you for your support of the author's rights. • Little, Brown and Company • Hachette Book Group • 237 Park Avenue, New York, NY 10017 • Visit our website at lb-kids.com • Little, Brown and Company is a division of Hachette Book Group, Inc. • The Little, Brown name and logo are trademarks of Hachette Book Group, Inc. • The publisher is not responsible for websites (or their content) that are not owned by the publisher. • First Edition: September 2014 • Library of Congress Control Number: 2014936772 • ISBN 978-0-316-32065-8 • 10 9 8 7 6 5 4 3 2 1 • WOR • Printed in the United States of America

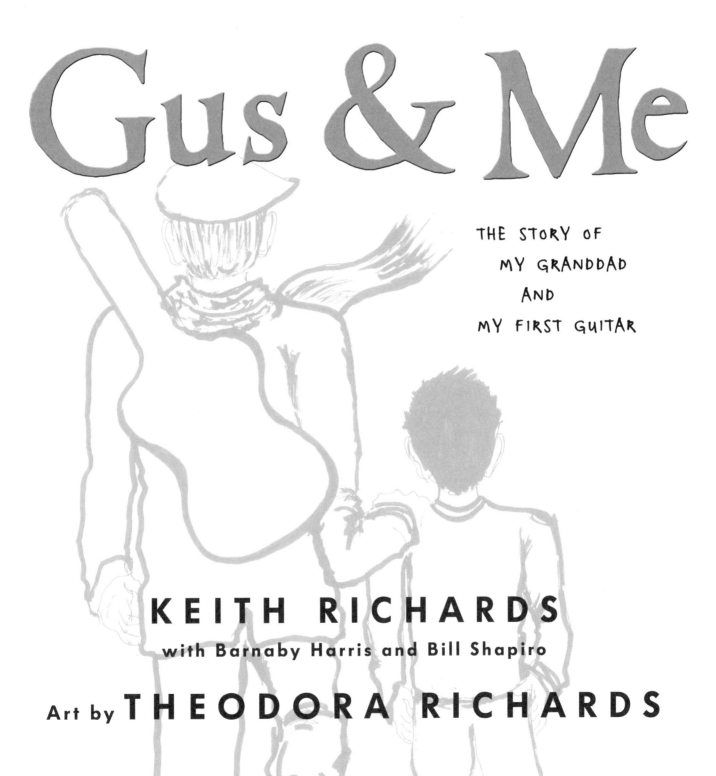

Gus & Me

THE STORY OF
MY GRANDDAD
AND
MY FIRST GUITAR

KEITH RICHARDS

with Barnaby Harris and Bill Shapiro

Art by **THEODORA RICHARDS**

Megan Tingley Books
LITTLE, BROWN AND COMPANY
New York   Boston

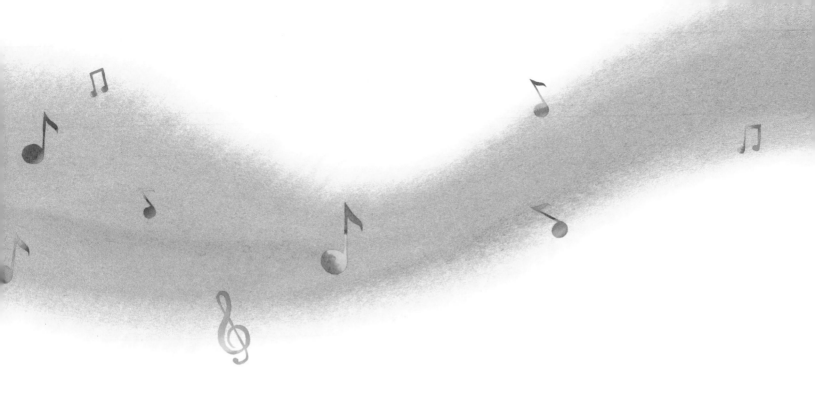

Gus & Me

THE STORY OF
MY GRANDDAD
AND
MY FIRST GUITAR

KEITH RICHARDS

with Barnaby Harris and Bill Shapiro

Art by THEODORA RICHARDS

Megan Tingley Books
LITTLE, BROWN AND COMPANY
New York   Boston

T heodore Augustus Dupree
lived with seven daughters near the Seven Sisters Road,
in a house that was filled with instruments and cake.

Theodore Augustus Dupree
could play the piano and scrape the violin,
blow the saxophone and strum the guitar.
He had been a soldier, a baker,
and the leader of a dance band.

SOLDIER

Baker

Leader of a Dance Band

But now Theodore Augustus Dupree was my granddad.

Now he was Gus.

There was nothing like visiting Gus.
The closer to his house I'd get,
the bigger my smile would grow.
By the time I landed on his doorstep,
I was all teeth.

He'd be waiting at the front door for me.

"*Fix the sink, Gus,*" my grandmother would call out.

"*Can't do, Emma,*" Gus would call back.

"*Keith and I are going for a walk.*"

He'd wink at me and whistle for Mr. Thompson Wooft,

and our adventure would begin.

Battersea Bridge

BIG BEN

Lord Nelson

We'd walk for miles.
We'd walk through towns,
and we'd walk through the countryside...
and Gus, he would hum every step of the way.
He'd hum whole symphonies as we strolled
from one village to the next.
He'd hum funny little tunes
as we wandered skinny streets and smoky alleys,
marching songs as we tiptoed around foggy ponds
and explored silent forests.

7 SISTERS ROAD

With Gus, you had no idea where you'd end up.

One time he led me all the way to the top of Primrose Hill
to look at the night stars.
"Don't know if we can make it home tonight," Gus said.
So we slept under a tree on the top of the hill,
with the sky lights above us and the city lights below.

Once Gus walked us all the way to London
and into the workshop of a big store
that sold instruments.

"Let's just pop in here. I've got to pick up some strings."

Inside, it looked like a beehive.

Gus lifted me up and sat me on a shelf

so that I could see everything.

Violins hung from the ceiling by wires.

Horns clung to the walls.

Men in long brown coats

fixed broken instruments and built new ones.

I watched as they bent over cellos, trombones, and trumpets.

They dabbed at the drums with glue

and tapped at them with tiny hammers.

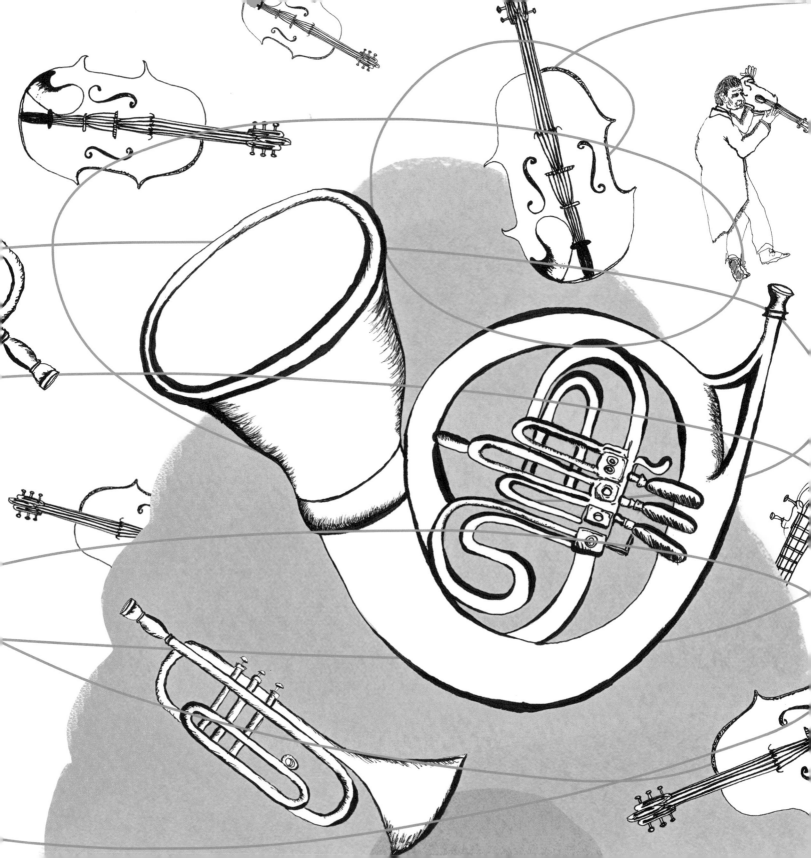

Men tested the guitar strings:

dinka-plink dinka-plink.

And the drums:

dok-dok fum-fum dok-fum.

DOK-DOK
FUM-FUM
DOK-FUM

My eyes followed a line of guitars
that snaked around the room on a conveyor belt.
And in the middle of everything,
big, bubbling buckets of glue went
blub blub blub.
It was magic.
I sat on that shelf, watching it all.

BLUB

BLUB

BLUB

BLUB

BLUB

BLUB

BLUB

BLUB

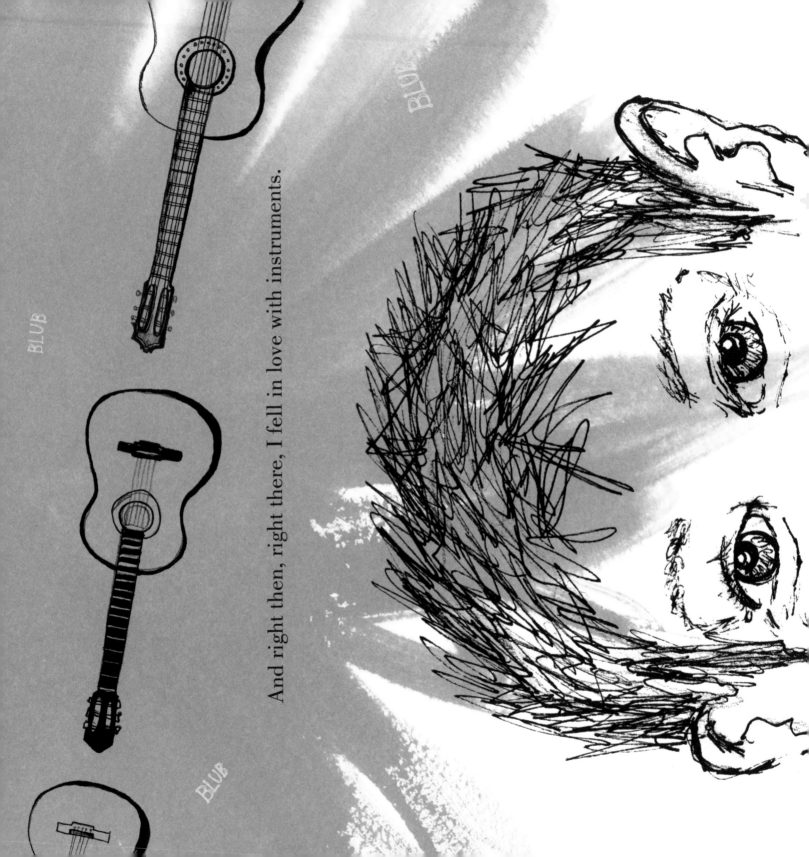

And right then, right there, I fell in love with instruments.

When Gus and I got back to his house that day,

I took a long look at that guitar

that always sat on top of his piano.

It seemed more beautiful than ever.

All I wanted was to make the strings go

dinka-plink-plink like the men in the store.

But I couldn't reach it.

"*When you're tall enough, you can have a go,*" Gus said.

Every time I visited Gus, I reached for that guitar.
Even on my toes, I couldn't touch it.

One day, I felt like I was tall enough to grab it,
but I didn't even have to try.
Gus simply handed it to me.
"All yours," he said.

He sat with me,

taught me how to hold it,

strum it, and pluck a little.

"When you learn how to play 'Malagueña,'"

he told me, *"you can play anything."*

Dinka-plink dinka-plink dinka-plink.

And I practiced and I practiced on that beautiful guitar.

DINKA PLINK
Dinka-Plink
DINKA-PLINK
DINKAPLINK
DINKA PLINK
DINKA-PLINK
Dinka-Plink
Dinka
DINKA-PLINK
DINKAPLINK
DINKA-PLINK
Dinka
DINKA PLINK
Dinka
Plink
DINKA-PLINK
DINKA PLINK
DINKA
Dinka
PLINK
Dinka-Plink
DINKA
PLINK
KA-Plink
DINKAPLINK
Dinka-Plink
DINKA
PLINK
DINKA-PLINK
KA-PLINK
DINKA PLINK
Dinka-Plink
DINKA-PLINK
DINKAPLI
-PLINK
Dinka
PLINK
DINKAPLINK
DINKA
PLINK
PLINK
DINKA PLINK
DINKA PLINK

One day, Gus heard me playing
"Malagueña," and he nodded.
Then he said something I'll never forget:
"I think you're getting the hang of it."

After that,
I took that guitar everywhere.
I went to sleep with my arms
wrapped around it.

Even today, all these years later, I think of Gus.

Every time I walk onstage, every time I write a song,

every time I reach for a guitar and play

a few *dinka-plink*s for my own grandchildren,

I say to myself,

Thanks Granddad
Thanks Gus!

ABOUT THIS BOOK

Creating the art for *Gus & Me* was a labor of love.
When researching the images for this project,

Theodora traveled to England,

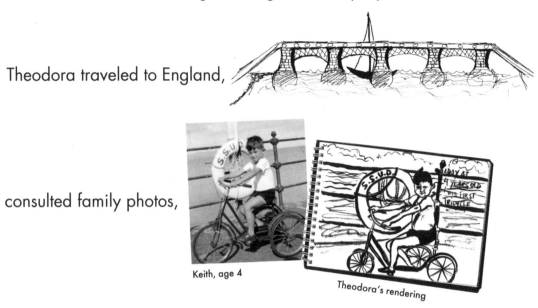

consulted family photos,

Keith, age 4

Theodora's rendering

and spoke with her father to draw on his memories.

Keith sketched the "beehive-like" music
shop as inspiration for Theodora.

This book was edited by Megan Tingley and Bethany Strout and designed by Gail Doobinin with art direction by Patti Ann Harris.
The production was supervised by Erika Schwartz, and the production editor was Christine Ma.
The illustrations for this book were done in pen, ink, and collage on paper. The text was set in Bodoni.
Theodora created the hand-lettered display type throughout the interior, except what is on pages 31 and 33, which were created by Keith.
The family photos are included courtesy of the Richards family.